Praise for Matthew Fonk

"I first did business with Matt when he owned a printing company. I found his attention to detail and follow-through to be exemplary. Since then I have watched his evolution in the real estate business. His integrity is above reproach, he is creative and constantly strives to improve himself and his business. I am happy to recommend Matt and Cavalier Estates LLC."

—*David Tilney,*
President at Keyper Corporation

"I know Matt to be a resourceful and reliable businessman. I have consulted with him on advanced trust strategies and investment projects and am impressed with his skills."

—*Jack Shea,*
Manager at Able Property Co

"Matt is excellent. I always get a quick response to any inquiry I make, and his direct dealings with my renters really takes the burden and hassle out of owning rental properties. He vets every tenant thoroughly, and I'm never worried that my properties are being damaged. I would highly recommend him for owners and tenants alike. Any problems at my properties are taken care of immediately."

—*Brooke Juan,*
Attorney & Rental Property Owner

"A good overview of property management with some great tips from a guy that has learned the business from the bottom up."

—*Gary Johnston,*
Financial Freedom Principles Semninars

PROPERTY MANAGEMENT

MATTHEW FONK

PROPERTY MANAGEMENT

A Guide for the DIY Manager
Don't let your rental properties crush you

Edited by Carol Ann Olson, Ph D.

D&OB
3959 Van Dyke Rd, Ste. 265
Lutz, FL 33558

Disclaimer:

This publication is designed to provide accurate and authoritative information in regard to the subject matter covered. It is sold with the understanding that neither the author nor the publisher is engaged in rendering legal, accounting, securities trading, or other professional services. If legal advice or other expert assistance is required, the services of a competent professsional person should be sought.

—From a Declaration of Principles Jointly Adopted by a Committee of the American Bar Association and a Committee of Publishers and Associations

Cover design by JT Lindroos

ISBN: 1-943402-30-2
ISBN-13: 978-1-943402-30-4

CONTENTS

Introduction   1

1. **The Property Manager**   3
The Role That is Performed

2. **How It started**   5
An Entrepreneurial Story

3. **Tenants**   13
The Good, the Bad and the Ugly

4. **Marketing**   31
Research, Setting Rents to Showings

5. **Maintenance**   45
Remodeling, Repairs, and Communications

6. **Reports**   59
The Tools That Help Make Decisions

7. **Legal and Compliance**   63
Ignorance of the Law

8. **Pets, Companion and Service Animals**   77
Are They Pets or Not

9. **Pest Service and Preventions**   87
The ABCs of Pests

Conclusion   99

INTRODUCTION

Rental Properties can be a great source of passive income if they are managed properly.

On the surface it seems very simple: buy a property, possibly fix it up, find tenants and collect the rent. What could be easier, right? Managing property can be very fulfilling, both from a financial and a personal basis. Every single day I get a sense of satisfaction knowing my company is providing a quality service. I consider my tenants to be part of my team, and I am proud to provide them with more than just a place to live. I provide them with quality places that they can call home.

There are many people with two, three or more properties who would like to make extra income from renting the properties out. When done correctly—which encompasses the understanding of all the ramifications, potential pitfalls and the legal aspects—it can provide the extra income that most people desire or need.

But be warned: managing property and handling tenants can be a lot of work. It is very fulfilling when done properly with the right systems in place. On the other hand, without a good understanding of everything involved and without those systems to make it all run smoothly, the fun can quickly dissipate and it can become a burden. Properties that are mismanaged will eat you alive.

That's where a good property management company can help. They can take over the day-to-day operations, put a system in place to make it all run smoothly, and allow you, the owner, to sit back and enjoy the profits.

This book can provide you with an understanding of what is involved in managing rental properties. Once you have finished, you will have enough information to decide if this is a task you want to tackle by yourself, or if it would make more sense to find a qualified, professional company to handle it for you.

This book is meant to provide useful information but not legal, accounting, or other professional services guidance. For those latter concerns, you should always find a good attorney, accountant, or other professional to help you out.

THE PROPERTY MANAGER
AND THE ROLE THEY PLAY

I have managed many properties over the years and have found that renting or leasing property that you own can result in good, consistent income along with a feeling of moral satisfaction from providing a safe and comfortable place for people to live. However, finding good tenants and managing the property can be extremely stressful, challenging, and filled with legal landmines.

As a landlord, you not only need to fill your properties with paying tenants. You also need to be concerned with maintenance, remodeling, pest control, collecting rent, landscaping and so forth. You need to be cognizant of legal issues involving eviction, the Americans with Disabilities Act, Service Animals, the Civil Rights Act, the Fair Housing Act, as well as the employment of contractors and possibly employees.

Whether you have just one property that you recently purchased or you own many units, hiring a good property manager can remove the burden of the day-to-day administration and the direct interface with tenants from your shoulders. This gives you something that cannot be recouped: your time to do with it what you will. And it allows you to enjoy a steady income stream. Time and money, what can be better than that?

In this book, I will outline key strategies and information about tenants, evictions, property, legal issues, insurance, pets, pests, managing staff and contractors.

You may realize that managing your rental property is not an easy task. There are many details to remember, pitfalls to avoid, and many dangers that you might just want to throw up your hands in frustration. The job of a property manager is to throw a lasso around all of the tasks, dangers, potential damages and difficulties to make your life easier and your income steady. This allows you to sit back and enjoy the many benefits and satis-factions of renting out your property. You can rest easy knowing you are providing quality housing for families so they can lead happier lives.

Let's get started!

Property Management Defined: The process of managing property that is available for lease by maintaining and handling all the day-to-day activities that are centered around the piece of real estate. Property management may involve seeking out tenants to occupy the space, collecting monthly rental payment, maintaining the property, and upkeep of the grounds. Apartment complexes are handled by some type of property management company.

MATTHEW FONK, ENTREPRENEUR

TIP: *"When you have something important, you need to stand on it, get on top of it and get it done. Be one step ahead of the rest. Be pro-active, work the problem personally until it is completely resolved using vendors or other parties. That's the type of person I am."*

I am the owner of Cavalier Estates, LLC, the premier property management company in the Tampa Bay area. I founded the company in 2006 to manage my own properties. I never imagined that my main objective would be to acquire long-term management positions for single-family homes in Tampa Bay and the surrounding areas.

I was introduced to the fascinating world of real estate at an early age. My father and I were walking in the neighborhood of the first house we lived in Camp Lake, Wisconsin when we met a guy who was fixing up a house and renting it out. He had two homes right next to each other: one to live in and one to rent out. I remember thinking, that was a really interesting way to make money and I guess it always stuck with me.

A few years later my parents built a home next to my grandparents' farm in Salem, Wisconsin. So in a sense, I grew up on a farm where I learned lessons that I have embraced through my entire life. One of the most important lessons was that you have to be able to fix things yourself. It's a protection against someone trying to take advantage of you. There are times when no one will come to your rescue when something is broken, so you have to be self-reliant and willing to get your hands dirty. Another lesson from the farm is that you must be able to work with people, not against them. Farming is dirty, laborious and sometimes dangerous work, and there is no room for anything but your best efforts.

When I was young, my parents split up and I eventually moved to a small town with my dad, which was more of a neighborhood than a farm community. The lessons I learned from my childhood on the farm, of cooperation, communication, and the willingness to jump in, stuck with me. I built upon these values to begin my own business at an early age.

That's where I got my entrepreneurial skills. Kids would come to me to get things fixed, which built up my character. I could be relied on to not only get it done but to get it done right. I got my start helping my friends in the neighborhood as well as the adults. I fixed broken bicycles and other equipment like lawn mowers, snow blowers, dirt bikes, snowmobiles, and sometimes cars. Once it got out that I could fix just about anything, I had more business than I knew what to do with. Even at that young age I was busy making money by using my drive, intelligence and mechanical skills to help people.

In fact, one of those early ventures was my lawn mower repair business. On trash day in the spring, I would bike the neighborhood looking for discarded lawn mowers. I would drag them home, tear into them, find the problem and repair them. Then I would sell them on our front lawn. The result was that, at twelve years old, I made two hundred and forty dollars during the summer, which was a fortune for me at the time.

When I was in high school, I would stop at the local gas station each morning to purchase a box of six *Nutty Bars* for $1, taking them to school to eat myself. However, fellow students would see me eating them and ask if they could buy one. I took on a new business of selling *Nutty Bars* for a dollar each. In the end, I invested one dollar to make five. I also worked on cars and motorcycles, earning extra money and a reputation for doing things right the first time. I thrived on finding out what people needed and provided a solution to help them achieve their goals. But I also learned not to go after the same fish as everyone else. A vital component of my philosophy is that big opportunities are obtained by looking at problems from different angles and viewpoints and coming up with unique solutions.

"When everyone is thinking the same, no one is thinking."

—*John Wooden, 1910*

After taking a printing class in high school, I decided I thoroughly enjoyed all aspects of it, including graphics and marketing. I worked a few hours each day going to classes and learning everything I could about this new subject. This opened the door to college, where I earned a Bachelor of Science and Technology degree, with a focus on printing and digital imaging, from the Pittsburg State University located in Pittsburg, Kansas.

After college, I moved to Kansas City, Kansas and began working for a company called Print Time as a customer service representative. This was an excellent first career job that allowed me to develop with the company's philosophy and systems. This is where I realized that systems, utilized properly, allow people to really enjoy what they do. I moved up quickly, advancing to a management trainee position where I continued honing my customer service skills. This promotion actually taught me how the systems worked from the ground up. After relocating with the company to Phoenix, and working several months in management, I realized that it was time to go into business for myself. A printing business!

In 1999, I partnered with Larry Olson, friend and mentor in both printing and real estate, to acquire an existing print shop. We carefully researched five different states in the country and finally settled on Florida. (Growing up in Wisconsin, I think you can understand why.) I sent out over a hundred and fifty letters to printing companies asking them if they ever thought about selling their business. And, if so, I was looking to buy one in the area. We received thirteen responses and made three offers. One of the companies accepted our seller carried finance offer and before long we owned a printing business. This new company opened its doors in 1999 and we stayed with it for nine years.

While I managed the print business, I always had it in the back of my mind that real estate could be a good income generator. I dabbled in it a little throughout my career and even took a few real estate seminars while still running the printing business. I specifically kept in mind the course I took from John Schaub, *Making It Big With Little Deals*, relating to single family home ownership. I would eventually start to put his principles to work.

In 2001, my life changed again when I met my wife. Our second date was immediately after

September 11, and we dated for three years before getting married. My wife became pregnant in 2007. And, as soon as I found out, I decided to sell the printing business. I spoke with my business partner and we both agreed to sell. We sold it in August of 2008, less than a month before the start of the Big Recession. That's what you call good timing!

I spent the next few years as a stay-at-home dad and found time to restore a motorcycle, a 1958 Harley Davidson Servi-Car. After a couple of years, I realized I was going out of my mind and missed interacting with people. At that point, I owned one rental property and it was eating me alive. After all was said and done, the house was costing me three hundred dollars a month. In other words, I was losing money. One day having coffee with my friend and mentor, Peter Fortunato, I asked for some advice. Peter simply said to either structure an opportunity that would allow me to use the house as a down payment for another investment or get more rentals to help cover the negative. I ended up getting more houses to help cover the negative which relieved the negative cash flow, and with time we were able to restructure the financing on this home.

I had created a company called Cavalier Estates in 2006, which specialized in rental properties. I thought we would perhaps pick up a home to remodel and sell from time to time. Who knows, maybe even pick up a couple of rental properties.

However, following Peter's suggestion, I devoted myself to make Cavalier Estates the premiere property management company in Tampa Bay. Before long, I had seven houses that I rented out. Since then it has grown into something much more.

At the beginning, I did everything myself. I performed the duties of marketer, broker, engineer, maid service and everything else that needed to be done. I grabbed whatever I could to build my business at the start since, if you have nothing to lose, you may as well go after everything until you can whittle your way into a better situation. I even remodeled houses myself. It's not something I would recommend but I had to do it then. This gave me the information I required when I hired someone to do the work I needed.

That's how I got into property management. It took me nine months to get my real estate license. I studied at home on the computer while changing diapers. You know, if you go to the class, there are instructors who will point you to what you need to know. It's far more difficult at home because you have to know the information cold. You are not fed the information that may be on the test. You have to know every aspect of real estate in order to pass.

Today I manage hundreds of properties all over the Tampa Bay area. The majority of my business comes via word of mouth and referrals. I know my business well, and so the owners and tenants have confidence in me and my abilities.

TENANTS

Tenant defined: pays periodic rent for a temporary right to occupy, possess, and/or use a property; the right having been granted by the property owner (landlord) through a lease or tenancy agreement.

Tenants are the lifeblood of this business. You cannot have an adversarial relationship with your tenants. I learned this from David Tilney, who is a master of this craft.

"Be hard on the problem, soft on the people."
—*Roger Fisher*

That's the way to grow and prosper in this business. So many managers want to go into defense mode when addressing an issue.

I remember a blog post from another manager where his tenant replaced all the appliances in the home. The manager was really upset that the tenant did this without permission. I responded to the blog post with something of the following: even though the tenant didn't get permission, I would recommend a face to face meeting. The idea is to see if they truly did enhance the property. Maybe they put the owner's appliances in storage until they move. Maybe they planned to leave the new appliances if they moved. Maybe they decided they never wanted to move again and that they would be life-long tenants. My point is that these types of tenants are the ones you want living in your home. They bring value. Jumping on a tenant for every little thing doesn't develop a good relationship. I try to look at situations from a business stand point of the owner. I truly believed the tenants here improved the value and didn't create more work for the manager or the owner. That's a bonus.

Central to my belief is that tenants are part of the team, and sometimes this means going beyond what is normally expected. I remember one tenant who needed some help recently after an apartment fire on Thanksgiving Day. The tenant was a nice lady who had lived there for quite a while. She didn't have renters insurance and had no place to stay while the unit was repaired. I put her up in another unit and gave her a few hundred dollars to help her out. She had always been a good tenant. She didn't cause problems and always paid her rent on time so I felt it was appropriate to give her a helping hand. Let this be a lesson to the tenant, to get renters insurance! It's worth every penny.

If you have systems in place that are designed to give the tenants what they need for everything regarding the house, then everything should roll smoothly. If the tenants are trying to buck the system with the right procedures, you'll be able to spot it right away and correct the issues.

When taking on new tenants, what concerns me is if they are going to be decent people and live in a home as if they were owners and part of the community. Communication is the key. I talk to tenants for about an hour during the leasing process so they understand everything and get their questions answered. I want to make sure they are people with real values. This is also the last interview before we handover the keys to the castle. Once they are tenants they are part of the team. Another way to look at the tenant is as an on-site manager for the house and grounds. We want our tenants to have pride in their new home.

Sometimes both parties realize that we are not the perfect fit for each other and go our separate ways. We had an applicant show up to the lease up with her adult son. He said he was moving in with his mom. We mentioned we had to run an application on him but he refused. So in the end we discussed why we were unable to rent to them. It was better to find this out before they moved in. It makes the situation much easier to deal with.

In my experience, the best thing any owner/property manager can ask for is quality tenants. These are the people who can make property management fun and fulfilling. They understand they have rights as a renter, but they also understand *their* responsibilities as well. You may find it tempting to focus on the problem tenants because they make trouble. But I've found that focusing energy and time on good tenants is always better in the long run.

My strategy is to encourage and support tenants who are responsible and treat the property as if it was their own. These tenants tend to stay longer, cause fewer problems thereby improving your profits and freeing up your time for other purposes.

Some of the habits of a good tenant include:

- They read the lease with us and ask questions to understand their lease.
- They follow the terms of their lease.
- They pay their rent on time.
- They rarely have difficulties with their neighbors.
- They treat their rental like it was their own property.
- If they have concerns, they make them known to the landlord in a timely and rational manner.

Problem tenants are often consistently late paying their rent, damaging the property, breaking the rental agreement in greater or lesser degree and generally don't get along well with their neighbors. I am always fascinated to find that bad tenants are often the biggest complainers and take up enormous amounts of my time and energy.

Putting the time into tenant selection is probably the No. 1 key to having a successful lease term. If you cut corners and go by gut feelings in this area, you will not like the outcome. Put in the time, have the tenant fill out a good application. Pull their background and credit references. Check their existing rental references. This will help you select the best of the best tenants for your home.

Signing Rental Agreements

The rental agreement or lease is the contract between the landlord and the tenants. This is a legal contract and contains the critical details of the arrangement between the two parties. The agreement outlines, among other things, the monthly amount of rent and the term of the rental period. This is the most important document since it spells out the 'meeting of the minds' in full between you and your tenants.

Obviously the agreement needs to include the monthly rent, as well as the terms of how and when it is paid. You might, for instance, state that rent must be paid online, by check or money order and not cash. Also, any late fees to be assessed for late payment of rent, grace periods and check rejection fees should also be documented.

Likewise, deposits and additional fees need to be written in the agreement. Include the amount of the security deposit and any limitations on its use. You should clearly outline exactly what will be sub-tracted from the deposit upon moving out, include-ing cleaning fees, repairing holes in walls and dam-ages from pets. It is a good idea to spell out how the deposit will be returned. Each state may require certain procedures to be followed within a time frame. This will help you legally when the tenant moves out and has a disagreement about how much of the deposit they receive back from you. Most important of all is to follow your state law.

The term of the agreement needs to be stated, as well as any conditions for early termination. For example, you may allow early termination with two months' notice. You could also state that the tenant is liable for the full amount of the rental agreement unless you can rent it out before the lease expires. But know your state laws in this area as some states require this clause to be outside the lease as a separate agreement. You can work with the vacat-ing tenant and let them help you show the property since they are the ones leaving before the end of the lease.

The names of all the tenants who will occupy the unit must be spelled out in the agreement. This includes the names of both members of a couple, whether married or not, any children and anyone else who will be living there. This is essential because this makes all of them financially responsible renters liable for the full amount of the rent regardless of circumstances. For example, if two people move in as roommates and one leaves, the one remaining must still pay the full monthly rent. Note that all parties are still responsible unless one releases the other with the landlord's approval. It's always best to get it in writing

The people listed on the rental agreement are the only people allowed to live in the dwelling other than a guest staying for a few days. Anyone who stays longer than three days must be screened if they want to be added to the agreement, which gives you a chance to do the standard credit and background checks, collect additional rent, and gives you the right to refuse to allow them to stay. Your lease should include language granting you the right to evict a tenant who moves in others without your permission.

The lease should also state whether the rental is month-to-month or for a fixed term.

A month-to-month agreement self-renews each month. However, I recommend long-term leases, as committed tenants are the best way to go.

Other things I have found valuable to include in a rental agreement are:

- Whether or not you allow pets. And, if so, any restrictions such as type or size.
- Clear verbiage stating that illegal activities, drug dealing and excessive noise are pro-hibited.

- Any rights you claim and circumstances for entering the property, as well as how you will notify the tenant.
- Any other limitations or restrictions.
- Whether or not a business may be run out of the unit.
- Tenant rights to the use of common areas such as pools, laundry rooms, etc.
- Hazardous recreational equipment such as a trampoline should be prohibited.

When the tenant signs the lease, I recommend you do it in person. This gives the tenant a chance to get his questions answered and for you to handle any concerns they may have. Each page of the lease should include a separate space for the tenant's initials or signature to provide proof that they read the whole document. Be sure to leave plenty of time for the tenant to read the entire agreement without rushing.

TIP: *"Spending your effort up front during the leasing process saves time which can help eliminate bad tenants and establishes good communication between all parties."*

Occasionally a tenant may request changes to the terms before they will sign the document. Whether or not to accept these changes is up to you. But if you do accept them, ensure the modification is mutually acceptable, fully described in the agreement, and signed by all parties. When granting lease changes to a tenant, keep in mind who is in charge. I advise against allowing changes to the lease terms.

The move in and move out processes are both important in getting the house turned for a tenant. Documentation is necessary for deposit or bonuses to be provided. If you are going to put in a claim against the deposit, there are rules that must be followed. Each state will have its own statute. But in Florida, I highly recommend that you include the deposit statute in the lease. This should spell out the following:

- The process on how the funds are held if you take deposits.
- How to submit a claim.
- How much time is allowed to submit the claim.
- How much time the tenant has to object to the claim.
- What happens if you do nothing and try to keep the money.

The move in and move out process can be simple if the tenants follow the lease, and the lease up meeting is the time to train your tenants. Don't wait until they give notice to discuss the move out process. Do this during the lease up. When they give notice, it is a great opportunity to remind them of their duties.

Credit, Background and Criminal Checks

Tenants need to turn out to be who they said they were on application. I recommend that you never accept a tenant until you have performed a full set of background checks, including verifying their credit, checking their criminal and sex offender history. I also call at least two previous landlords for tenancy history as well as their current employer to verify income. I always call at least the last two landlords because the most recent one may give a good reference because he's trying to get rid of the tenant. When all this is said and done, a tenant is not approved until the lease up process is completed which means money is exchanged and the lease is signed.

First you must get the appropriate information from the tenants. This includes their names, previous addresses, driver's license numbers, previous landlords and bank account numbers. The information is to be supplied for *everyone, ages 18 and up,* who will be residing in the rental home. Be sure to get each tenant to sign a form indicating it is acceptable for you to perform these background checks.

The credit history will give you an idea of how well they pay their bills. You should run a credit report from all three bureaus: Equifax, TransUnion and Experian. The information in these reports paints a very clear picture of your tenant's credit-worthiness.

- Do they pay their bills on time or are they habitually late?
- Do they have foreclosures or bankruptcies? (I have found that people with foreclosures often make great tenants since they have owned property before but just can't manage the financial burden.)
- Does their record include any evictions?
- What is their credit score?
- Any other information about their creditworthiness. Keep in mind that some-times no credit is great credit.

The background checks, including their criminal and sex offender histories, will help you determine if the tenant is a high risk. There are any number of tenant screening companies available who can gather this information for you for a small fee. And, it is common practice to pass this fee on to the tenant up front, non-refundable.

Naturally you should contact previous landlords to talk to them about how well the tenant behaved, how they paid their rent, the condition of the unit upon move-out and so forth. Finally, call their place of employment to verify their income.

Once you have all of this information, you can make a decision about whether or not to allow the tenants to move into the unit. Remember, you should take into account the background of all tenants over the age of eighteen in the unit since all of them are responsible.

Evictions

The worst job of an owner/property manager is to evict someone from the property. I have had to file very few evictions, yet they are always challenging, time consuming and gut wrenching. Some of the reasons you would evict someone include:

- The tenant has violated the lease agreement in a non-trivial manner, e.g., the tenant has a dog yet the lease states that no pets are allowed.
- The rent is not paid on time, especially if the tenant is habitually late.
- The tenant damages the property well beyond normal wear and tear.
- The property is being used by the tenant for illegal purposes.

You cannot evict someone because they have reported housing code violations or they sued you for violating discrimination laws. You also may not harass a tenant to try to get them to leave. This means you cannot change the locks or cut off the utilities.

Those few times I have had to do an eviction it has gone more or less smoothly because I always ensure I have a proper paper trail. You must have documentation showing the problem, any attempts to resolve the issue and so forth. This becomes critically important if the eviction results in a lawsuit. Courts generally want to see facts in writing and having all your ducks in a row will increase the likelihood of your success should the eviction go in that direction.

Once you have determined you have cause for an eviction, you cannot just remove the tenant yourself. You have to file a lawsuit to get a court order for the eviction and you may need to pay the sheriff to come out and remove the tenant. That can result in fees anywhere from five to six hundred dollars. If the tenant contests your eviction, you can spend thousands. Once the tenant has been removed from the house, it's best to remove all their belongings at the same time, leaving the home empty of all items.

A method that I have used in the past with great success is to talk to the tenant and make him an offer to leave. You could offer him *cash for key*, a few hundred dollars (or some other incentive) to vacate the premises and leave the place broom-clean with all their belongings gone. This saves the time and hassle of going to court, getting the sheriff to come by, hiring people to move the belongings out to the street and hiring a handyman to clean up the place. A settlement will not only reduce your hassle but it could also prevent a lawsuit down the road.

Another interesting tip I learned recently was to have the tenants agree to move out by a said date, and to have the tenant write on a sheet of paper that they would agree to continue to make payments to you for the balance of the lease after they move out. They may not make the payments but then you can possibly get a judgment for the note they gave promising to pay you. You avoid the eviction cost and still can get a judgment.

Handling the Problem Tenant

TIP: *"I do have to say tenants can do some crazy stuff from time to time."*

Even though you've done your best to screen your tenants beforehand, sometimes problems do occur. Some of the issues that can happen include:

- Always paying the rent late.
- Arguing with everything.
- Damaging the property.
- Painting the walls strange glow-in-the-dark colors.
- Letting their animals run around outside without a leash.
- Moving in guests for long periods of time.

- The heavier problems of crime, drugs and gangs.

The saying "if it's not written it's not true" is a good adage to follow when managing property. Thus, it is very important that you have a written policy in addition to the terms of the lease. This can simply be a list of do's and don'ts to be given to each tenant when they move into the unit. By putting this list in writing you can help ensure there are fewer misunderstandings. If the tenant does cause problems, you can point to the list and use it to help enforce the rules or to aid in an eviction if it comes down to that.

The wisest policy is to follow the terms of your lease and other written documentation as closely as you can. If a tenant violates the rules you should immediately let them know what they've done and take the appropriate action. For example, if the rent is late then follow your policy. If you charge a late fee after the tenant is three days late, then *always* charge that late fee with no exceptions. If you don't allow pets and you find a tenant has a pet, jump on that problem and handle it immediately.

I've learned through experience that by following my own rules to the letter and keeping to my enforcement policy, I cannot be accused of favoritism or being unfair. I'm being totally fair since I am treating everyone exactly the same.

Of course if all else fails and you have tenants

that simply will not follow the rules even after you've followed your procedures, then do not hesitate to evict them if you are unable to negotiate the move out. It sounds heartless but if they are not paying their rent or are causing problems severe enough that you are impacted, you need to get them out of your life.

Occasionally tenants will attempt to move in additional guests or tenants for the long term (more than 72 hours for example) without permission. Sometimes they get away with this and there's nothing much that can be done about it. They might have a friend down on their luck or a relative who needs a place to stay while looking for a job. Of course the better tenants will come forward and will work with you.

Lease agreements should include a clause which states that when there is an increase in the number of people staying in a unit for more than 3 days, you charge the tenant an extra hundred dollars a month per person. That's on top of their normal rent. The additional people also must go through the normal vetting process and be approved before they can stay longer than seven days. It might seem odd that you would charge extra for additional people living in a unit, but there is extra wear and tear on the unit from the additional people.

The way I handle this situation is to tell the tenant they should think about charging their guest or guests rent, say two or three hundred dollars a month each. That covers the extra hundred dollars rent they will owe plus helps with the hassle of having more bodies in the same space. It also gives them a little bit of compensation for their efforts. I really don't want extra people moving in. But if I can get my tenants to admit they would like to move another resident in, we can run our background checks and properly approve the additional tenant.

MARKETING

TIP: *"Your goal when you acquire a property to manage is to put in the effort up front so you don't have to deal with it day in and day out down the road."*

Determining the Right Price for Rentals

TIP: *"The rental price is not set arbitrarily. Market conditions determine the price of rental housing."*

The price of a rental unit is not arbitrarily set by the owner or the property manager. I've learned through experience and created a method that works for determining the rental price. By following this method you will be renting the unit faster and have a higher likelihood of attracting longer term tenants.

The rule is that market conditions determine the price that can be charged for rental property. Your job when setting the price is to research those conditions, and generally the proper amount becomes clear after the research has been completed.

Obviously you should know the condition and

specifications of the home to be rented. You'll need to know things like:

- The square footage of the home which is used to figure out the price per foot.
- How many bedrooms, baths and so forth? You can put a value on an extra bedroom or bath.
- Whether or not there is a garage, and if not, what is available for parking.
- Does it have a deck, carpet, tile, granite counters? Is it newer? HVAC, ceiling fans, security lights and alarm? These little perks can make a tenant excited.
- Does the home have a pool and is it private or part of a common area?
- Any other features such as a sprinkler system.
- Is the home prettier or uglier than others in the area? Curb appeal is money.

Next, I look around to see if there are any properties for rent in the neighborhood. Generally I limit the search to about a mile in all directions. You can use online rental advertising services and classifieds for this search and you can even drive through the neighborhood yourself to take a look. I've often spoken with the neighbors to find out what they know about the area and any rental information they may have. You'd be surprised what the locals see and hear, and they are often a great source of information.

Find those properties that are similar to yours, e.g., those that have the same number of rooms and bathrooms. Note the prices, without making any judgments, for each of the units that match your criteria. Now make a list of those properties itemizing:

- The location of each one.
- The advertised rental amount; look at the cost per foot and the rents based on number of beds and baths.
- The number of bedrooms, baths and garages.
- Any other significant features such as a deck, sprinkler system, pool, fenced yards.
- How long the units have been on the market.
- How quickly they are renting.

From this exercise you should be able to come up with a range of rental prices for homes similar to your own. Set the price between the ranges you found from your research. Lower the price under the following conditions:

- If there are a lot of homes similar to yours for rent in the area and
- If your home must be rented quickly.

I've found it best to set the amount just below the median price in the area in order to attract long term tenants. If you set the price too high, few tenants will apply. Conversely, if the price is too low, you'll find yourself not only inundated with applications but they will also be of lesser quality.

As you advertise the property you'll need to keep an eye on how many people are making inquiries. If the number is low you may need to adjust your price down a bit, and if a large number of people are calling, you might want to bump the price up.

I recommend posting the price on a sign at the property. Sites such as Craigslist allow anyone to post ads. Someone can swipe your ad, lower the price and create a false value to make people bite. These scammers ask people to send them the deposit in advance to hold the unit and then disappear.

Advertising for Tenants

TIP: *"The idea is not to get just any tenant. Anyone can do that. What you need to do is get the RIGHT tenant. You want people who will treat the property as their own, do much of their own maintenance and improvements and who believe they are part of my team."*

My advertising procedure is to place a sign in the window and on the front lawn of the unit in addition to using the media. If you have a property controlled by a Home Owners Association (HOA), check with them for appropriate procedures. I generally wait until I have all of the information about the property, including the price, before I sit down and write a really nice advertisement. The ad needs to promote the property and make it look very attractive. Point out any advantages to the property itself, such as a pool, as well as anything special about the location. You might say, for example, that the unit is close to public transportation, schools, and a shopping center. Highlight anything that would make the property more attractive to potential tenants.

Of course the advertisement also needs to include, at minimum, the price, a description of the property, number of bedrooms and baths, and the location. Include anything the tenant needs to know about the unit. Always include plenty of good photos of the unit and its features. If the previous tenants agree and their belongings look good, ask if you can use photos of the unit with their property inside. This allows a prospective tenant to see how the rooms may hold their belongings.

One point I want to stress is to check and double check the contact phone number in the ad. I remember once I placed an advertisement and wondered why I didn't receive any calls from anyone no matter what I did. It turned out the phone number was wrong by one digit. I wasted weeks of effort because of that one simple mistake. So check that number!

In addition, verify that the ad is running as expected and is accurate in every place you've set it to be run. If you put an advertisement in the local newspaper, be sure to check that out regularly. Check the advertising and MLS websites. Note that the internet is free and statistically more people search on mobile devices every day. When you advertise, know your market and place your ads accordingly.

Before the ad runs, be sure to tidy up the home and ensure it is ready to be rented. I like to make sure it is white glove clean, meaning literally every surface is spotless. All repairs should be done and anything that was broken should be fixed before any prospective tenant sees the unit. Also, and this is very important, make sure the unit smells good and also, place a floor mat in the entrance area and a 'welcome' mat at the front door.

Set the temperature between 78 and 85 degrees in the summer and between 55 and 60 degrees in the winter. This leaves the air conditioning on in the summer to prevent moisture (and possibly mold) and the heater on in the winter to prevent the pipes from freezing.

You might want to stage a few things to make the unit look more attractive. A bottle of wine or vase full of flowers in the kitchen or a basket of potpourri in the bathrooms is a minor cost and has a real impact on making the place look better. Just remember, sparkling homes rent fast.

One unhappy fact that I touched on previously is that you have to be aware of the scams that occur. Sometimes you'll find that your photos have been stolen along with the text of the ad and a fake email address. The people who write these ads will try and rent the property for far lower than the actual price, and they will ask people to send them money directly. Of course any money sent to the scammers will be lost. I recommend that you put a watermark on all photos to help deter these scammers. Post a window flyer at the property with the rental price and your contact information. You will find out very quickly who has been seeing a false advertisement.

A while ago, a lady called me asking when she could move into a unit. I was surprised because this was the first time I had heard from her. She explained that she responded to an ad, sent the initial deposits and rent, but never heard back. When I inquired further, she said she was from out of state, and hadn't seen the house in Florida. Upon investigation, it turned out that a scammer had taken someone's advertisement but had somehow connected me to the property and stolen the poor lady's money. She was very angry but there was nothing I could do.

You may also receive calls from people who want to send a check as a deposit. They'll send too much money, then ask you to send the difference back to them in cash or wire transfer. The first check will bounce and you'll lose the cash you sent back. It is a sad fact that you always need to be on the lookout for scammers trying to fool you. A good rule to follow is if it seems too good to be true it probably is a scam.

Showing and Renting the Property

TIP: *"Spend the time up front during the vetting process, including credit and background checks, to be sure your tenant is a good fit for your property and will take responsibility for the unit. Spending the effort early in the process lets you sit back and enjoy. Otherwise you are putting your energy back into the problem time and again."*

If you hire a property manager, let the manager do his/her job. It's very important that all showings of the property and rental negotiations be done by the manager. This not only prevents you the owner from bypassing the manager's procedures, but it can keep you out of trouble. Most owners are not aware of the law regarding fair housing and discrimination. Letting the manager do his job allows you the owner to relax and get paid.

I've found it best to set up a 24/7 answering machine because you never know when a prospective tenant will call. The answering machine should include a way to sort the incoming calls to make it easier for you to respond to them appropriately. Use a dedicated line for this so nothing gets in the way of the prospects getting through. Check the calls once or twice a day to stay on top of the rental prospects.

Use a written script when describing rentals so you don't change the verbiage from prospect to prospect. If you answer from memory, information may be forgotten or changed, which can be embarrassing, lose prospects or worse yet, result in violations of laws and regulations.

As you start talking to prospects, don't negotiate or discuss rental terms other than the agreement length, facts about the property and the advertised price. Nothing else should be discussed until the rental application and disclosure forms have been signed. This ensures that you are treating each tenant the same and you are following all applicable laws regarding housing. Also, be sure and collect the application and background check fee before you perform the various background and credit checks.

Applicants are prescreened using the information in the rental application. You screen based upon how much income they have, their background, employment, rental history and how long they intend to remain in the unit. This prevents you from spending a lot of time and effort on prospects that do not measure up to your standards or meet your qualifications.

The following information is used in the screening process:

- A credit report is always obtained and reviewed.
- The past and present landlords are called to verify that proper notice was given, rent was paid on time and the property was well maintained. You'll also want to ask other questions about non-sufficient funds checks, why the tenants are vacating, was the security deposit returned in full and if not, why not, and so forth. Have a good conversation with these earlier landlords to get as much information as you can.
- Look over the background checks to ensure the prospect does not have a major criminal record and is not a sexual predator. It's important to understand that sexual predator is NOT a protected class for discrimination purposes (believe it or not this may change).
- Check the past and present employers to verify income. Generally you want to ensure the prospect has income of at least three times the rent.
- Advise the potential tenant of any parking restrictions.

- While talking to the applicant, make note of any derogatory comments they make about their previous landlords and employers. These are possible red flags for problems down the road.
- Always follow the applicable fair housing and other laws during these discussions.

There are many other criteria to consider during the screening process. Remember, the idea is to screen out tenants who are going to have problems paying the rent, will not be responsible for the property and who may have criminal or other serious issues of concern.

When a tenant is disqualified because of credit information contained in a credit report, it is necessary that they be sent a letter. This is required by the Fair Credit Reporting Act.

Once you've screened the applicant, it's time to set an appointment to execute the rental agreement. Be sure you have a well drafted, fully vetted agreement that complies with all appropriate laws.

The property manager should schedule an appointment so the applicant has enough time to review the entire contract and get any questions or concerns answered. Generally you should allow one to two hours. Go through the entire contract with the applicant prior to letting them sign it.

During this process I've found it's wise to keep my eyes and ears open. Listen to what they say and examine their appearance. Following your gut can come into play at this point. This is the final step before you've committed to the rental and it is your last chance to screen out any prospects that may not work out. It is far better to screen out an applicant, even at this late stage, then it is to have to evict them further down the road.

I will stress again to pay attention to your gut, sixth sense, or whatever you want to call it. If you are getting a bad feeling about the prospect then, at the very least, have a longer conversation with them to appease your feelings. There are plenty of other people looking for a place to live and it is far better to delay than it is to accept a bad tenant. There have been a few times during a lease up that I just got up and walked out. Example: the son told me that he would be living in the unit and wouldn't be on the lease. I just didn't want that hassle. Example: I had a family who wanted a really nice home. But when they came to the lease up, only the husband was willing to sign the lease; the wife refused. So I declined to rent them the house. Point being, the manager must have control or he/she will fail.

It is important not to take the unit off the market until you have signed agreements and you have received the tenant's payment. Depending on how close it is to the move in date, you should collect all funds in certified checks, money orders or cashier's checks. You shouldn't accept personal checks or credit card payments. You should also confirm that all utilities are paid and in the tenant's name as well as utility deposits. Confirming/encouraging that the tenant has secured renters insurance is essential as well. After that, all that is left is to shake your tenants' hand and give them the keys to the unit.

MAINTENANCE

It is a fact of life that property of any kind requires maintenance from time-to-time due to normal wear-and-tear at the very least. Weather can cause damage such as mildew and water stains, pipes can leak and carpets can get dirty or torn. Even units that are not occupied can show damage or require maintenance from time to time.

I had a unit that was sitting idle for two months. The tenants rented the place early to secure it but couldn't move in right away. No one lived on the property and the doors were not opened during that entire time. I was glad I did an inspection just before they arrived, because the toilets had built up rings from the standing water and one of the faucets had sprung a leak. This damage occurred even though no one lived in the place for two whole months!

TIP: *"The manager should use the time when the tenants are there to sign the rental agreement as a maintenance training session. This will let the tenants know what aspects of maintenance they can perform themselves and what parts should be sent to the property manager."*

As a property manager, one of your prime tasks is to shift some of the responsibility for maintenance over to the tenant. I've always found that tenants are very willing to fix the smaller problems themselves once they understand that this helps keep their rental price low.

Preventive maintenance is done whenever the property manager feels that it is in his/her own best interest to have it done. Generally I have found it best to schedule it between October and January; cooler months for indoor/outdoor work like gutter inspection, roof repair, A/C check, etc. You can tune the systems for winter if you like.

Something I have learned through long experience is that tenants love to hear that they are doing a great job. Thus you should occasionally let them know when you catch them doing something right. I remember driving by a unit once and noticing that the yard was being very well maintained. I made it a point, right then and there, to stop and let the tenant know. They were thrilled with the feedback!

Little things like that can really help in keeping your tenants happy and will reinforce the good job they have been doing.

I want to stress that the idea of preventive maintenance serves several purposes.

- Obviously you want to prevent problems from happening.
- Prevent small problems such as cracks in the paint from becoming big problems like water getting into the walls causing mildew.
- Document that safety issues have been inspected and corrected if needed to protect against possible lawsuits.
- Verify that the tenant is keeping up his maintenance responsibilities.
- Gently remind the tenants of their maintenance responsibilities.
- Make sure areas where the tenant should not be allowed are locked. For example, attic access shouldn't be allowed and the attic should be locked because the tenants can fall through the ceiling.
- Secure stoves to the walls since children can open oven doors and stand on them. They could be killed if the stove were to fall on them.

Schedule a time when the tenant will be home to perform the maintenance and inspection. This allows you to fulfill one of the biggest objectives, which is to educate or reorient the tenants about their responsibilities for maintenance. If the tenant is not present during the inspection, you should schedule a time to get together with them to perform this educational step.

Some of the tasks, and this list is by no means all-inclusive, that need to be done when doing preventive maintenance are described below.

- Over time, leaves and debris fall into the gutters and drainpipes of a house. This can cause water to back up and damage the unit. During preventive maintenance, clean these out to prevent problems.
- Filters on the furnace, air conditioning and dehumidifier units need to be changed once in a while, because the build-up of dust causes the motors to work harder and uses more electricity. Do this during your maintenance period, and be sure to let the tenant know the size of the filters so he can maintain them himself later.
- Smoke detectors can save the lives of your tenants, so make sure the tenant is maintaining them as per the lease agreement.
- A properly maintained fire extinguisher also can save your tenants lives, and may help them put out a fire before it causes major damage. If the tenants have extinguishers,

you might remind them that they need to be maintained on a regular basis.

- I recommend that your rental contract include a provision making smoke detectors, carbon monoxide detectors and fire extinguishers the tenant's responsibility to maintain if your state allows this. If you do this, be sure to remind them during the preventive maintenance.

- Problems with plumbing which are not addressed in a timely manner can cause major issues. Be sure and include plumbing inspections in your preventive maintenance plan.

- Make sure any railings on the stairs are tight and secure as loose railings can be a safety hazard.

- Check and fix any gas lines and connectors to the water heater and furnace.

- Look at door knobs, seals, window locks, blinds and screens.

- Make sure the yard is being kept up.

Document everything you inspect and any damage that is corrected, having the tenant sign off as well. I had a tenant who tried to sue because she claimed she slipped and twisted her ankle due to a loose railing on the stairs. Since I always kept excellent records of all preventive maintenance, I was able to get the suit dismissed because I could demonstrate that the railings had been inspected and found to be tight and secure. If I had not had that documentation, she may very well have won damages.

Other areas you should inspect include those listed below. Note the condition and, if needed, schedule any repairs that are needed.

- The condition of the paint is important not just because peeling paint looks bad, but because the paint acts as a layer of protection from the elements. Cracks in the paint can allow water into places where it should not be, which can cause damage.
- Any house built before 1978 must be inspected for lead paint if any maintenance occurs. You need to know the law regarding lead paint as the rules are complex and the fines are steep.
- How is the water drainage? Water should drain away from the property. Also, water should not build up in standing, stagnant pools, as these are breeding grounds for mosquitoes.
- Any oil or cracks in the driveway, walkways or garage floors?
- Look over the yard to see how the bushes and trees are trimmed and the general condition of the landscaping and such. It is impor-

tant that the exterior yard look good and be well maintained.

- Do all the exterior lights work properly? While this is generally the tenants' responsibility, it's a good time to check them out.
- The condition of the flooring and/or carpeting should be noted.
- Problems in fireplaces can quickly become safety issues as smoke and fire can damage the unit and put the tenant at risk. So check those fireplaces for cracks and damage, and make sure the tenant has them swept as needed.
- Mildew can be a big problem if not discovered and corrected. Check the wall colors and conditions and note any signs of mildew or leaks. If you suspect mold, call a professional company to check it out.

There are many other things you can and should inspect when you perform preventive maintenance on a unit. Remember you are not just looking for obvious damage, but also for safety issues and signs that damage will occur down the road. Thus a water stain on the wall might be simple to correct now but if left unattended could lead to a very expensive job if the stain results in mold.

If mold is found, it's just best to have it professionally handled. Otherwise it could be expensive. Most people have found from their searches on the web that bleach can kill mold. This is true to a limited extent, but bleach will not penetrate porous surfaces such as wood. Vinegar and peroxide can help to prevent it from coming back, but these chemicals do not penetrate into wood and similar surfaces. Again, my advice is to hire a professional who can completely handle the problem so it does not come back.

Remodels

TIP: *"If a unit looks rundown and is in need of remodeling in order to make it more desirable for the tenants, it is well worth the investment of time, money, and sweat equity because it will rent out quicker and at a higher monthly price."*

Every once in a while a unit will need to be remodeled. Most often this occurs immediately after an owner signs up for property management, although it can happen anytime. A remodel requires a significant amount of time and effort, often making the unit unavailable for days at a time. Thus it is best to schedule remodels between tenants if at all possible.

When I remodel a property, I make sure it comes out more desirable and nicer than before. If a unit seems small, I might knock down a wall or put in a window or two. If the kitchen cabinets are worn out, I might replace them. I might replace worn countertops with granite tops, depending on the size of the kitchen. Small kitchens with granite look spacious. If the fixtures are old and costly to repair, I'll replace them all.

This brings me to the second point of remodeling: to reduce the costs of upkeep. This is the time when you'd consider replacing all of the fixtures in the bathrooms, especially if you've been getting hit with large repair bills because of leaky pipes.

The best rooms to focus on during remodels are the bathroom and the kitchen. People look at these first when they enter a dwelling. If the kitchen looks like it was built a hundred years ago, it's time to replace it with a more modern look and feel. If the bathrooms are so dirty they make those in a truck stop look good, well, then fix them up. These are the most used rooms in any home and the most likely to suffer damage (water, smoke and even fire) while occupied.

Obviously check over the walls and paint them if needed (filling in any holes, of course), and change out or thoroughly clean the carpets. Clean carpets and freshly painted walls will make a unit look brand new. If possible, I recommend you remove any carpet and install a very nice tile, as this will last longer and will be less prone to damage.

Repairs

TIP: *"It is very easy to sell tenants on the idea of being responsible and doing most normal repairs themselves. You just have to make sure they understand that rents will be higher if the property manager has to fix every little thing that breaks."*

I use independent contractors for repairs and preventive maintenance. For repairs, the best solution is to get the tenant to cover the first seventy-five dollars of the bill as kind of a deductible. I have found this gives them an incentive for doing the work themselves or hiring someone on their own to get the repair taken care of, especially for smaller problems. You do have to remember to include this in the rental agreement, and it has to be discussed at the time the agreement is signed.

Once the tenant enters a work order into the web site, it flows through my system. The appropriate contractor is selected based upon the type of work to be performed. Thus a plumber will be required to fix a leak in a pipe while a carpenter might be needed to repair damage to cabinets.

You should have agreements set up in advance with all contractors that you need on a regular basis. You must set these up in advance, as you need to thoroughly vet them all before allowing them to perform any work. You must perform reference, background and criminal checks on all contractors before allowing them anywhere near a unit.

I was told of a property manager, whom I shall not name for obvious reasons, who hired a contractor without checking his background. The contractor did the work but it was substandard and had to be completely torn out and redone a month later. This tripled the cost of what was a relatively minor problem simply because the property manager hadn't bothered to check references.

I've heard of situations where a contractor was hired quickly, again without background checks, and it turned out they had employees with criminal convictions. Since these contractors had access to the tenant's property they were able to steal quite a few things before being caught. Save yourself a lot of trouble by vetting your contractors!

Make it the responsibility of the contractor to call the tenant to schedule an appointment for getting the work done. This removes the property manager from the middle. Believe me, you don't want to be negotiating between the tenant and the contractor for dates and times. Save yourself a hassle and leave that between them.

Tenant Portal for Reporting Problems

TIP: *"One of the best time savers of all is to automate the handling of work orders from*

beginning to end using a web-based appli-
cation."

The best systems are automatic, meaning they function day in and day out doing the administrative tasks for you. This frees up your time so you can focus on the more important aspects of the business. Additionally, by using an automated system, there will be less errors, your tenants will get service faster, and you can produce reports to help you keep an eye on things.

All service calls must be logged even if the tenant reports them directly to you or your office. Sometimes a tenant will walk in the front door or call on the phone to complain about an issue. In those cases just log into your online property management system and make the entries just as if the tenant did it himself. This way the problem will run through the system in exactly the same way as if the tenant logged into the web site.

The automated system accepts the work order, with all of the details of the problem, directly from the tenant. Since this is on the web it allows the work order to be created twenty-four hours a day, seven days a week. It doesn't matter if it's a holiday, a weekend or late at night. When the problem is on the tenant's mind he can log into the system and enter the data. Of course this doesn't mean the problem is addressed during those off-hours, but at least the tenants can write up the work order whenever they desire. They will receive an email indicating their work order has been accepted by the system.

Once the work order has been entered into the system by the tenant, it automatically runs through a standard work flow. From the work order, calls can be made to the contractor to perform the work, follow-up calls can be scheduled, and then it can be closed. Of course, once it is closed the tenant will receive a final email telling them the work has been done.

REPORTS TO HELP
YOU MANAGE THE PROPERTY

TIP: *"One of the best reasons for using an automated property management system is they allow you to produce reports on demand. So when your property owners call wanting information you can deliver them nice reports telling them exactly what they need to know."*

One of the great advantages of using an automated property management system is the sheer volume of reports that you can generate at any time. Some of the reports that you can get from any property management system include the following:

- Property listings.
- Customer listings.
- Lease expirations.
- Security deposits.
- Delinquencies.
- Move in dates.
- Move out dates.
- Work order statistics.
- Vacancies.
- Charges paid.

- Deposit breakdown.

The property management system that you choose will have dozens more reports available at your fingertips. You should expect to be able to get most of these reports for the current month, for historical months (past months), and for three to twelve months in the future.

Your property management system should also include normal accounting reports such as:

- Various general ledger reports.
- Aged receivables (detailed and summary).
- Profit and loss statements.
- Yearly budgets.
- Balance sheet.
- Cash flow reports.
- Rental unit profit and loss reports.

As you can see, the property management system you choose should automate all of the back office functions as well as provide all of the reports that you will need to run the business.

I have found that an excellent purpose for some of these reporting functions is to be able to see property performance data at a glance. When I get a call from an owner who has a question or wants to "see the books", it is a simple matter to email or print out the appropriate reports. This way there is no scrambling around, no panic while searching for data and no hedging on the questions. You simply retrieve the appropriate report, review it and send it off.

LEGAL AND COMPLIANCE

This section is intended for informational purposes to demonstrate some of the legal complexities of managing property. I am not a lawyer. You should engage the appropriate legal services to help with your own situation.

TIP: *"Don't pull any old lease off the shelf, don't go borrow a lease your friend uses, and don't go downloading a template from the Internet. Draft a lease specifically for your property and the municipality in which the property resides."*

In my experience, thoroughly understanding the legal aspects of property management makes a huge difference in providing for a smoothly run operation. Your state's Landlord Tenant Law should be read yearly.

You need to understand rental agreements, the Americans with Disabilities Act (ADA), the Civil Rights Act and the Fair Housing Act at the very least. You also need to have a thorough understanding of the local and state laws which affect property, rentals, housing and construction, to name a few.

Some of the legal procedures you need to understand include the following:

- For any significant construction, you need to understand permitting requirements.
- If you are hiring contractors, you need to understand the laws in that area.
- If you have employees, you must have a thorough understanding of how to hire, fire, pay and discipline them as well as deal with injury liability issues.
- You need to understand the inner workings of rental and lease agreements.
- You have to be thoroughly grounded in the Fair Housing Act and the Americans with Disabilities Act.
- If you allow any kind of pets, you must understand the liability ramifications.
- You must understand the ins and outs of eviction procedure.

These are just a few of the legalities that you'll need to understand completely in order to manage properties.

Many properties are governed by the additional rules and regulations of the HOA. You must make absolutely sure that you master and follow these provisions as HOA's are often not very forgiving of transgressions against the rules. These may govern how the property is advertised, what kind of and when maintenance may be performed.

Evictions serve as a prime example of how complex these legalities can become. You have to do evictions exactly right. If you make mistakes, you will cost yourself time, money and you may be on the wrong end of a lawsuit.

When you want to evict someone you must have cause and that must be documented in writing. Tenants have certain rights and because of that you have to be able to demonstrate to a judge that you've given them the appropriate opportunities to address the situation. You must give three days' notice, for example, so they have a chance to get caught up on the rent.

It is critical that all email messages and voicemails be kept on file. You'd be amazed at the things tenants write in emails or leave on an answering machine. All of this information may be used to support your case for eviction.

Once you are sure you have your ducks in a row, you have to fill out some forms and go before a judge to get a court order for an eviction. This is done in a special emergency procedure designed specifically for evictions. If you make any kind of mistake, the judge may toss it all out and order you to go through the whole thing again, which includes paying the fees once more. An error that I ran into once was starting the three-day notice on a court holiday. The judge threw it out and ordered the process start from the beginning. That was an expensive lesson. You'll want to hire a process server so the eviction is served right, and you'll need to hire the sheriff to get the people out of the unit (you never do this yourself).

I've learned it is always better to communicate with the tenant before you perform an eviction. I try to come to some kind of agreement that causes them to leave without going through the eviction process, which saves money, time and aggravation.

TIP: *"Sometimes cash for keys is fast cash for a fast move!"*

I'll point out that an eviction goes on the tenants' record, for example, and that it will be more difficult for them rent in the future, especially in nicer properties. I may offer them a few hundred dollars if they leave the place broom clean and empty so I don't have to hire someone to clean up and remove their property. There are multiple options available but at times you need to be creative. My methods work great for me and have saved me from the hassles and expenses of going through the eviction procedures. Believe me, it is worth it because evictions are one of the most traumatic aspects of being a property manager.

Rental Agreements

TIP: *"Spend as much time as you need on the rental (lease) agreement. Time spent here will pay off over and over again and eliminate many potential problems. On the other hand, not doing a good job on this agreement is a sure-fire way to guarantee that you and your tenants will not have a pleasant experience down the road."*

One of the most important legal documents in the armory of the property manager is the rental or lease agreement (referred to as the rental agreement from here on out). These documents must be done right since they are the basic agreement between you and your tenants. I discussed the rental agreement earlier, but feel it is such an important document that I'm going to discuss it again.

Don't go to some website and use a boilerplate rental agreement. Don't swipe one from some other complex, and don't use the one your friend let you borrow. None of these will work well because the agreement must be tailored to your municipality, your state, your circumstances and your system.

If you don't know how to put a lease together or you are unsure of yourself in this area, hire an attorney. Make sure he or she is a real estate attorney who specializes in this kind of law. Sometimes novice property managers think they can get their rental agreement drawn up by any type of attorney they find. Unfortunately, property management is so complex and convoluted that this would be a mistake. Most states allow an owner/principal write their own rental agreement. Again, make sure you understand the law here. Some specific clauses may be required in the contract.

If you did write the rental agreement yourself, get it vetted by an attorney specializing in real estate. Again, go with the expert in this field.

TIP: *"The rental agreement is the playbook governing the relationship between the tenants and the property manager. It is the most important document between the two parties and you should treat it as such"*

In some states, if your rental agreement is for less than six months, you may have to charge sales tax in addition to the rent. This demonstrates how complex it can be to manage property. The various legalities all need to be properly addressed.

Everything about the relationship between your tenants and you must be spelled out in the rental agreement. I take the attitude that if something is not in the agreement, it is not true and certainly isn't enforceable. Make sure your tenants understand and acknowledge this fact. On those occasions when something does change later, you need to make sure the rental agreement is modified using a written addendum. This way any disputes can be resolved just by seeing what was documented.

The rental agreement specifies the date it becomes active and names all parties, including the property manager (landlord) and all tenants occupying the unit. It is vital to include ALL tenants in the agreement, because if any leave, you want to ensure those remaining are still responsible for the rent and all other terms in the contract.

Include the term of the lease, noting that a longer term is always better than a short term. I prefer a one-year lease with an option to renew. In fact, my agreement allows the tenant to pay the equivalent of one months' current rent to guarantee they have the option to continue their lease when one year is up. This amount is a fee, not a deposit or rent and is not refundable. It simply holds the home for them at the end of the lease so they can make the decision to stay for additional year with the rent locked (i.e., not to increase by a certain percentage) for the next term.

You also should spell out any possible dangers, such as radon gas and lead paint (on houses built before 1978) so the tenant is aware of them. Include any informational pages and brochures to educate your tenants. I include a mold addendum as well as a bedbug addendum so the tenant understands about their responsibilities in these areas. The lead paint laws are very complex. Assuming your property is older than 1978, I would advise you to get the appropriate training on how to deal with it. A mistake here can be very costly. Learn here: http://www2.epa.gov/lead/renovation-repair-and-painting-program-property-managers.

I give each tenant a very long checklist, ten pages, and ask them to go through the whole thing within three days of moving into the unit. This check sheet notes every single feature of the property and has room for notes and check boxes to indicate whether the feature is good or needs attention. Believe it or not, virtually every tenant takes the time to go through this entire form in detail. That's because I stress to them that this is their opportunity to get anything fixed that got missed during my inspections, and they know they will be responsible for anything they forget to note.

I always do a thorough inspection of any property before it is rented, and I often have others inspect as well. I might ask an electrician to inspect the wiring or a plumber to inspect the pipes, depending upon what repairs were done, the age and condition of the unit, and what problems were reported in the past.

But as I point out to the new tenants, things sometimes get missed. I might have opened a drawer, closed it too hard and broke something. Something in the back of a cabinet might have been missed or a pipe might have sprung a leak after the inspection. At this point, it is the tenants' chance to rectify, at my expense, anything that needs to be corrected. After three days they lose that opportunity. This is important because you don't want a tenant who has damaged a unit to claim the damage was there at the beginning.

American with Disabilities Act, Signed into law July 26, 1990

TIP: *"When remodeling we consider making the property ADA compliant. Not only does this make good business sense, because it increases the number of tenants available to rent, but I feel it is just the right thing to do."*

The ADA is an extremely comprehensive law which guarantees the civil rights of people with disabilities. The purpose of this act is to ensure that someone who has a disability of some sort has the same opportunities in life as everyone else in the United States. It is designed to protect their rights to employment, purchase goods and services, and to take advantage of government programs at the federal, state and local levels.

To be protected under ADA, a person must have a disability, which is loosely defined by the law as a substantial limitation to one or more of life's activities due to physical or mental impairment. It also protects not only against actual impairments, but even someone who is perceived as having impairments.

Many property managers do not like to advertise they are ADA compliant. I guess they feel it's too much of a liability or they don't understand the law. My own opinion is if the home allows for ADA compliance, go ahead and advertise. After all, it means there are more tenants who might apply for the unit. Remember, you are not *required* to rent to someone just because they are disabled. You *are* required to give them the same opportunity to rent the home as anyone else.

If you have a no pets policy for your homes, service or companion animals must be exempt from this policy. You can't deny any person the use of his or her guide dog. It's not ethical and it's illegal. A companion animal, by the way, is also any animal such as a cat or dog, which is prescribed to aid a person who has emotional or mental distress. For example, a veteran who just came back from Afghanistan might require a dog to help with his stress, or someone who was an alcoholic might need a cat to help with the cravings.

I've run across many individuals who pretend they have service or companion animals when in reality they have no such thing. The animal must have been trained to support the disabled person in some way. You have the right to ask for certification from a doctor and for proof that the animal has been properly trained. Note that this paper work is available online allowing tenants to bluff their assertion. While it happens, it's highly recommended not to fight this as well.

I like to allow for ADA access, and my goal is that most of my properties will be ADA compliant. For example, when I remodel a unit, I ensure that the doors are widened to allow for wheelchair access. Not only is it the right thing to do to support those with disabilities, but it considerably increases the pool of tenants who might rent the unit.

As I've said before in this book, it is always best to get long-term tenants. This significantly reduces costs because you don't have to keep advertising and repairing the units. In my experience, when a tenant who is disabled moves into a property, they tend to remain for a long time. This is great for all parties, as I get a long term lease and they have a great place to live.

You have to be careful, though, when showing your property to those with disabilities. You don't question them about their impairments. For instance, I heard of one landlord who was showing a place to a wheelchair bound gentleman who wanted to be on the third floor. The landlord took it upon himself to advise the prospect that he wouldn't be able to access the unit. You don't tell an impaired person what they can or can't do. Instead, let the prospective tenant make the choice.

You may be surprised when they stand up out of a wheelchair.

According to ADA, you have to let those with disabilities make whatever modifications they need to have access to your property. You don't, however, have to pay for it. So the best strategy is to show your property to the prospective tenants and answer their questions. If they tell you they need a ramp for their wheelchair or special filters for their asthma, well, that's fine. They can get those modifications made so they can lead a normal life, at their expense. In addition, when they move out, they are required to pay to remove those modifications if necessary.

My advice is to support ADA fully, and to be completely aware of the rules and regulations. That way you will be helping those who have disabilities, increasing your pool of possible tenants, and avoid possible lawsuits for discrimination.

Again, you are not *required* to rent to disabled individuals if they don't meet the qualifications. The requirement is that you treat them the same as everyone else, and allow them to make modifications to support their disability. Thus if a disabled tenant does not meet your income standard or fails the background checks, it is perfectly acceptable to deny their application. Just be sure, as always, that everything is documented in writing.

Fair Housing Act and the Civil Rights Act

TIP: *"If you are going to be a property manager, even if you only rent out a single unit, you'd better know the Fair Housing Act inside and out. Running afoul of these laws can cost you money, time, and hassle. Knowing these laws inside and out will prevent successful lawsuits against you and much aggravation."*

The Fair Housing Act (FHA) was introduced in 1968 and was heavily amended in 1988. These laws were designed to protect the civil rights of renters and homeowners based upon several different criteria.

Basically, you cannot discriminate against a potential or actual tenant based upon race, color, national origin, religion, sex, familial status or handicap. In other words, you must treat people the same when considering their rental application.

The following are some acts of conduct that are prohibited based upon any of the protected classes by the FHA.

- Refusal to rent the unit.
- Refusal to negotiate.
- Making the unit unavailable.
- Denying the unit.
- Setting different terms or conditions.

- Steering them to different units.

You may also not discriminate or take any action of any kind against someone who reported you for violations of the FHA.

You must be careful when communicating with your tenants or prospective tenants to avoid violating the FHA rules. One common mistake that I learned while having a conversation with another property manager is asking about children. You cannot ask tenants if they have children; they can volunteer the information. But if you ask and later deny their application, they can potentially sue under the FHA.

Thus, you have to be especially careful in casual conversations to stay away from the protected classes. Make it a ritual to not bring up or discuss any topics related to those classes. Don't ask if someone is single or divorced, for example, as you could be shown to have discriminated because of that.

The FHA is very complex and you should get the appropriate training and legal advice to ensure you fully understand it and all of its ramifications to your business. That understanding could mean the difference between you losing time, money and sleep over lawsuits or a more stress free life. Education is fuel for your success. Try to keep on top of all rules and laws by attending local training opportunities to refine your system.

PETS

TIPS: *"I tend to be very cautious when allowing pets. I don't allow aggressive breeds of dogs, such as Pit Bulls. Also, all pets need a weight limit. I don't allow exotic animals or snakes either. The philosophy: if pets are allowed at all, is to have animals which will not damage the property or harm others."*

Pets can provide companionship, love and can be wonderful to have around. Properly cared for, they are a joy to individuals. Smaller dogs and cats are good companions and their very presence and unconditional love often make people feel better.

In general, I don't like to allow animals in my rental properties. There are just too many liabilities attached to having pets on the premises. This is from a legal standpoint as well as the fact that animals can cause damage to the property.

Of course, service and companion animals must be allowed because of the ADA. Often, a person's well-being depends upon these animals. So it is the right thing to do to give them a place to live along with the dog or cat they need to survive to have a higher quality of life.

As I said earlier in this book, I've had some problems with prospective tenants who falsely claimed their pet was a companion animal. When I asked for evidence of the fact, a doctor's order and phone number so I could ask them about it, the tenant admitted they were lying. If you don't allow pets, you have to be careful because this kind of thing happens occasionally.

Special Problems Presented by Pets

TIP: *"The biggest problem in Florida is pet liability. If the insurance companies find the wrong type of dog on the property they may cancel your liability insurance. Then if the dog bites or scratches somebody the owner and everyone involved can be liable."*

While animals can be wonderful to have in a home, they can also cause problems and may even be dangerous to the property, other tenants, and guests. Even pets which are properly cared for can, under some conditions, become a menace to others.

All animals, regardless of species, breed or size, can damage the property. They can scratch the wood, bite the walls, chew up the carpets and tear holes in things. Large dogs can create immense amounts of damage. Cats will scratch doors and anything else they can find.

Animals have waste products which can, if not

properly cleaned up, be both unsightly and a hazard. People can slip and fall on feces, bring it into their homes on their shoes, and it can attract insects and other pests.

When not properly cared for, animals can become a menace or even worse. Dogs let loose can bite tenants and guests; cats can bite and scratch; fish tanks can leak or burst. Other animals such as rodents can get loose and cause an infestation.

All cats urinate outside their cat box on occasion. Even a well-trained cat will miss sometimes or have an accident now and then. Cats which are not well-trained or have a urinary tract infection will urinate everywhere. Tenants who are not very responsible will forget to change the litter, causing the cat to look elsewhere to do its business.

The thing about cat urine is that it smells horrible, seeps through the carpets and can be almost impossible to completely clean up. Male cats which are not neutered will spray (urinate) on just about everything to mark their territories. Dogs also urinate inside the property, regardless of whether the tenants are aware of it or not. This stains carpets, walls and flooring, and even cement. Once urine, from either cats or dogs, seeps through the carpets, it gets into the wood beneath and becomes very difficult to remove. One unit was so badly damaged by dog urine that I had to scrape the surface off of a step that the animal had soaked.

Some tenants are allergic to animals, especially

cats, which means when you allow a tenant to move in with animals you may lose another because of harmful physical reactions. Of course this is only an issue if the units are close together.

Dogs often bark, especially the more hyperactive breeds, and can disturb the neighbors. If the neighbors are your tenants, this can cause them to move out prematurely. It can also result in calls to the police.

Birds produce special problems. Even though locked in a birdcage, their droppings wind up everywhere around the birdcage, all over the floors, counters and furniture in the vicinity. Their droppings usually get into the carpets where it is almost impossible to clean up.

And snakes, no way. Here's a sad story. In July 2009, a couple kept a python in their house and it got out and killed a two-year-old little girl (Associated Press, 2009). The risk of snakes is just too much for my properties.

Advantages of Allowing Pets

In spite of all the disadvantages of allowing tenants to own pets, there are many reasons why you might want to consider it. Responsible pet owners can be very beneficial as tenants. You just have to judge if the advantages outweigh the disadvantages.

While there is some debate about this, a few studies have shown that those who own pets often tend to stay longer because of the difficulties of finding pet friendly properties. Long-term tenants make a property manager's life easier because they save the costs of relisting the property, remodeling, cleaning up between tenants and so forth.

Dogs are good guardians and can help lower crime in a neighborhood. Very little scares away criminals faster than a barking dog.

Between thirty and fifty percent of people own a pet of one sort or another. By allowing pets you increase the number of potential tenants for your property.

You can also charge more for rent if you allow pets, especially if there are not a lot of pet friendly properties in your area. Some property managers add a small surcharge to each monthly rent payment for each pet, and many also charge a pet deposit to cover potential damages.

Studies have found that pet owners have higher incomes, which again increases the potential pool of tenants. You just have to be sure to always check their credit reports because a higher income does not necessarily mean they pay their bills and rent on time.

Animals tend to make people happy, and happy tenants tend to be more responsible towards your property because it feels more like a home instead of just a place to stay.

Insurance and Liability Issues

TIP: *"There was one case recently where two pit bulls were locked in a cage in a bedroom. A kid who didn't even live on the property let the dogs out of the cage. The dogs attacked and killed the child (Examiner, 2014). Even though the landlord had absolutely nothing to do with this incident he could have been sued."*

One of the huge problems with allowing tenants to have pets, especially dogs, is if the pet injures someone. The landlord may be held liable under some conditions. This is in addition to or instead of the pet owner being liable for the damage. You should note that bites are not the cause of most dog-related lawsuits. Many are from the dog jumping on someone, which scares them and causes the person to fall unexpectedly.

Generally, if a dog bites or jumps on someone, the tenant is liable unless the landlord knew the dog was dangerous and didn't have it removed. Of course the building owner's liability insurance may cover the dog. Courts may hold you, the owner or property manager, liable under the following conditions:

- The landlord knew the animal was a danger and did not have it removed, and

- The landlord had some control over the animal.

I require my tenants who have pets to get a liability policy on their animal. There are many companies that will provide this kind of insurance. I've found nine in the Florida area, for example. These policies are not cheap. But if the tenants really do want that dog, they will be willing to pay the extra cost. It is vital that the property management company be listed as additionally insured.

I guarantee that if a tenant's dog goes out and bites somebody, the lawyers are going to be all over you, the property manager or the owner. The attorneys see the house and they will come after the owner because the owner has the deeper pockets.

As an example of pet liability, in a Kentucky court case, the judge ruled that a landlord can potentially be held liable when a tenant's dog bites someone. If the landlord knew about the dog, he may be liable even if he did not give or revoke permission for the dog to be on the property (Justia U.S. Law, 2012).

Allowing Tenants to Have Pets

TIP: *"Pets are serious. Make sure you know what you are getting, make sure your insurances are in place, make sure you are named, make sure you are covered, and do a pet interview before you rent to them and you might be able to sleep better at night."*

If you do want to allow pets on your properties, ensure you've got a good pet policy. This needs to be incorporated into the lease or rental agreement, either directly or as an addendum. The addendum must be signed by all tenants living in the property.

Some of the things you should include in your pet addendum are as the follows:

- The tenant agrees to clean up after the pet both inside and outside the property.
- Extra rent (and deposit if that's what you want) shall be paid.
- Tenants will repair any damage caused by the pet at their own expense.
- That the pet will be under tenant control at all times.
- Give the property manager the right to inspect the pet and property with sufficient notice.
- Tenants will purchase pet liability insurance and name the property owner as additionally insured.
- Any offspring from pets violate the agreement.

- Any pests that result from the pets (fleas for instance) will be exterminated at the tenant's cost.
- Excess noise, barking, disturbances and threatening behavior (or, obviously, actual attacks) may be cause for withdrawing consent for allowing pets, and the lease may be terminated for cause.
- You might want to ensure any cats are spayed or neutered.

It is a good idea to include a weight limit for animals. For example, like me, you might want to allow dogs only under twenty-five pounds. Also, I recommend that you make it clear in the section about pets in the agreement that tenants are not allowed to babysit friend's pets.

I recommend that you charge extra for each pet, twenty to fifty dollars a month. Keep it reasonable but put the charge there. I don't charge a pet deposit, instead preferring to charge a larger pet rental fee. In the long run, charging more for pets will offset future damage costs.

You should always ask the tenants to let you do a pet interview so you can meet the animal (or animals) and determine for yourself if this is a pet you want to allow on your property. You need to see the pet and ensure it is not dangerous to other people, the property, or other pets.

To be completely safe, make sure the tenants

have properly vaccinated the animals, that they have the appropriate licenses, if applicable, and that the pets wear some kind of identification. Asking that all dogs have dog tags is entirely reasonable.

Remember, there is no requirement that you allow pets, excluding service and companion animals. You can ask all the questions you want and set any number of requirements you feel are necessary before allowing pets onto the premises. This is one of those things that is entirely up to you as a property manager.

One last note on companion animals and insurance companies. If an insurance company gives you, the owner, any grief about canceling the insurance on the property because the tenants have pets, just inform your agent that it's a service animal, etc., and provide documentation. That should help resolve the issue.

PESTS

TIP: *"I make sure the property is completely free of pests before the tenant moves in, no matter how much effort is involved. That way, if pests are reported by the tenant I know they either brought them with them or they came later."*

When tenants are responsible, there are rarely infestations of insects or rodents. Taking out the trash regularly, ensuring the dirty dishes are washed on a daily basis and cleaning up spilled food will prevent most creatures from deciding a home is a banquet hall. The outside of the property must also be kept clean of debris and trash and any maintenance issues that expose wood or leak water must be handled quickly.

On the other hand, when a tenant is sloppy or doesn't keep the property clean and well maintained, insects, rodents and other creatures will be attracted. These animals are searching for food, warmth, water and secluded places to build their nests, hives, dens or whatever is applicable.

In my properties, I ensure that, before a tenant moves in, the place is completely bug and rodent free. An exterminator is hired to spray as many times as needed and to examine for many different kinds of pests. When this process is complete, I am absolutely sure the properties are free and clear of infestations. This is vital as tenants may find insects and other pests after they move into a property. Because I've been careful to ensure the place is completely pest free, I'm confident these subsequent pests came with the tenant.

Something to always keep in mind about various pests is that the problem is not just that they are unsightly. Pests often carry diseases, some of them very dangerous or even fatal, and their feces can also be the source of bacteria and viruses. Quite a few people have very strong allergic reactions to the droppings, hair and body parts of various insects and animals.

My rental agreement includes wording which makes handling most pests the responsibility of the tenant. This gives the tenant some incentive to keep the place clean, pick up the trash and reduce the desirability of their home to these unwanted guests.

Different Types of Pests

Ants

These insects are attracted by water and food, like many other pests. When a tenant doesn't clean up regularly, leaves food on the floor or has piles of unwashed dishes, ants may appear. They get in through just about any pinprick of a hole and, once they find what they are looking for, it can be a real hassle to get rid of them.

Ants don't generally carry diseases, but many species can sting human beings. The sting of some species of ants produces red welts and a lot of pain. One thing ants love is soft, moist wood, so they may burrow into windowsills and baseboards if conditions are right.

To get rid of ants, you'll need to call in a specialist who will determine how the ants are getting into the property. Any cracks or holes will need to be sealed and the species of ant identified so the proper bait can be found. Spraying for ants is often not very effective, as the colony may be outside. You need to use bait containing poison, which is carried by the ants into their colony.

Bedbugs

Bedbugs are the bane of a property manager's existence. They feed off human blood and their bites, often found on the arms and legs, will itch like crazy. Bedbugs will be brought into a property in beds, laundry and luggage. Unlike most insect pests, bedbugs do not carry any diseases, but they sure can cause a panic.

An adult bedbug is about the size of a small seed, like those of an orange or an apple. Their bodies are flat. But after feeding, they swell up and change color to a red hue. Their eggs look like specks of dust and are almost impossible to see.

It is very difficult to eliminate bedbugs once a property is infested. You have to call in a professsional who will assess the situation then come up with a plan. Generally a professional will use fans and a heat source to heat the room to one hundred and eighteen degrees for at least thirty minutes. You have to allow more time so the *whole room and all of the belongings in that room* remain at that temperature for at least that long. This is needed to ensure all of the eggs are killed.

Bees

Sometimes honey bees will swarm and the whole hive will appear in the eaves or on the wall of a property. Carpenter bees will burrow into wood to create their nests. These insects don't carry diseases but many people are allergic to their stings. On some people, a single bee sting can result in death. Thus infestations of bees must be handled promptly.

Carpenter bees can destroy a property because they burrow into the wood in much the same way as termites. These bees attack unpainted soft wood. Thus if a tenant has damaged the property such that wood is exposed (even if this is just letting the paint peel off), the bees may take up residence. If you find out there is a carpenter bee infestation, you must call in professional help.

Honey bees look for a safe place for their hive

which is their home. If there is a hole in the roof or wall that leads to the attic, the bees may come inside and take up residence. Bees are killed by spraying with insecticide, but this is best done by a professional. Sometimes there are a lot of bees and finding them all can be a significant amount of work. In addition, the cracks and holes the bees used to find their way inside the property must be covered up.

Cockroaches

TIP: *"Cockroach infestations require multiple sprayings because, while the chemicals kill the adults, they do not affect the eggs. Thus two, three, or even four sprayings are necessary to completely eradicate them."*

These fast and seemingly intelligent insects are major disease carriers. They have been linked to over thirty different illnesses, including salmonella, staphylococcus, streptococcus and even polio. They love warm environments (over seventy degrees) with a good water supply and food which is easily accessible. Of course this describes most kitchens and bathrooms.

Not only do cockroaches carry diseases, but their feces, saliva and other body parts are also a major source of allergies for many people. These trigger allergic reactions, most often to children.

During the interview process, I will ask prospective tenants if they have ever had cockroaches. I know I've thoroughly had the property cleaned of all pests. So regardless of their answer, if cockroaches appear, they came with the new tenants. Cockroaches love electronics, especially microwave ovens, and that is how they often come into a home.

Drain flies

If you see swarms of tiny flies around the sink or shower, your property may be infested by drain flies (also known as drain gnats.) These tiny flies breed and live inside drains, in the organic material that sticks to the side of the pipes. This gunk is the breeding ground and food supply of these flies.

To prevent drain flies, the pipes need to be cleaned occasionally. All hair and gunk should be removed. Once there is an infestation, it can be handled by cleaning the pipes thoroughly and applying bleach or drain cleaner once a day for a week. Multiple applications are required to handle the eggs of the insects which have not yet hatched.

Pigeons

These messy, smelly birds leave droppings everywhere they roost. These droppings carry disease and produce very bad odors, as well as being unsightly. The feathers of pigeons often are full of mites, which can produce allergic reactions in some people. Once these mites get into a home, they can be difficult to eliminate.

Another fact about pigeons is that whole communities of them, sometimes dozens of birds, can congregate around a property. They are noisy animals and large numbers of them can be very disruptive.

If there is a pigeon infestation, any nests will need to be destroyed and the area must be completely cleaned and washed. Special spikes designed to prevent birds from landing can be placed in strategic places to keep them away.

Rodents (Rats and Mice)

One of the absolute worst infestation for many reasons is rodents, which includes mice and rats. Rodents spread diseases including the plague, Lyme disease, salmonella, rat-bite fever and many others. These are not minor ailments either, as agony or death can result.

Rodents eat any food they can find, chew on electrical wires and wood, create holes in the walls, and urinate and defecate throughout the home where they have taken up residence. They get in through holes in the walls (or make holes with their teeth), cracks and crevices.

Since rodents are looking for food and water, the best way to prevent their infestation is to take out the trash regularly, don't let the dishes pile up and keep the property clean. When cleaning to prevent infestations, you have to clean behind the refrigerator, stove and any place else where food can drop.

To handle infestations of rodents, a professional needs to be called. He will examine the property and seal any holes and cracks where the animals may be getting inside. He will then set traps with poisoned bait to kill the mice and rats. The poisons used to handle rodents can be deadly to humans so caution must be used. This is one area where a professional really needs to be called in.

Silverfish

These small, silvery insects don't carry diseases and don't cause any other significant health problems. They tend to be very shy creatures, living in piles of dead leaves or in other dark, moist places. These insects can cause quite a bit of damage within a home as they will eat sugar, paper, books, glue, clothing and many other items.

The best prevention is to run a dehumidifier. The insects prefer damp, moist air. Also, leaks need to be repaired quickly and standing water eliminated. Keeping the home clean, inside and out, will tend to discourage silverfish by removing sources of water and food.

Silverfish can be killed by any number of insecticides. Larger infestations may need to be handled by a professional exterminator.

Termites

Termites eat wood and can completely destroy a house if not handled. They will feed on the foundations of a home, as well as shelves, furniture, books and anything else made of wood or wood products.

Termites are attracted to moisture. To help keep them away, the tenant should keep faucets and water pipes properly repaired. Any standing water needs to be eliminated, the gutters must be clean, and any other place where water can accumulate needs to be corrected.

The other item that attracts termites is food, in this case anything made of wood. Firewood should not be stored in the crawl space of a home or near the foundation. Any wood debris needs to be cleaned up. Of course, any damage, such as missing paint on wood, should be fixed as quickly as possible.

If a termite infestation is discovered, you will need a professional exterminator.

Wasps

Hornets, yellow jackets and wasps are predatory insects which feed on other insects in the environment. They are very beneficial to humans because they help control insect pests and they also pollinate plants as well. On the other hand, wasps and hornets can produce a nasty sting to a human.

These stings can produce allergic reactions in some people.

Wasps and hornets do not normally spread disease. They occasionally will create small, paper nests on the eaves of a home. If the nests are easily reachable from ground level, it is relatively simple for anyone to use an insecticide to kill them all. Nests which are out of reach or larger may require a professional exterminator.

Other Pests

A property may be infested by many other pests as well. For example, raccoons and possums can be attracted to open garbage cans. These animals generally keep to themselves but, if cornered or startled, can scratch and bite. As with all wild animals, they may carry parasites and diseases.

Moths can infest clothing within closets and dressers, flies will take up residence in exposed garbage, and feral cats can find a home in just about any small place they can find.

Each of these infestations is easily prevented and inexpensively handled if they are taken care of quickly. When the property is dirty or untidy, insects and rodents may not be noticed until there is a major infestation requiring professional help.

Of course the worst tenant is the one who has infestations but either ignores them or does not want to take any responsibility to get them taken care of. It is rare but sometimes, when a tenant leaves a property, the work of the exterminator and maintenance crews can be extreme.

Preventing Pests

It should be pretty obvious by now that the way to prevent pests, for the most part, is to be responsible and properly maintain the property. Thus when I rent out a property, I ensure it is pest free before the tenant moves in. Doing so is responsible so tenants can rest assured they are not sharing their domicile with bugs and other critters. The second part of my responsibility as a property manager is to ensure the property is completely clean, I call it *white glove clean*, before a tenant even sees the place.

Responsible tenants keep properties clean. They don't let garbage pile up for days on end. They clear leaves and debris from near a house and don't let the dirty dishes sit in the sink for long periods of time. If they have pets, animals wastes are cleaned up immediately. They take care of any maintenance issues in a quick and efficient manner or report them to the property manager before small annoyances become large problems.

In other words, the key to preventing or at least reducing pests from infesting a property is to be responsible. Pests usually don't "just happen," and they almost certainly don't get to the level of an infestation "just because." Poor sanitary habits, lack of cleaning, and allowing the buildup of trash and filth are the causes, for the most part, and these are easily prevented.

CONCLUSION

"Property Management is an art and a science."

—David Tilney

I trust that this book has helped you understand what is involved in managing rental property. Of course this is only an overview of the information needed; there is much more to learn about the subject. There are many good books and articles available, plus quite a few quality courses and seminars to help you gain a deeper knowledge of this subject.

The most ideal properties to own and manage are single family homes. In my experience these are, by far, the best real estate investments you can make. Apartments have people above, below, to the right and to the left, and there are always issues among them. Condominiums are a headache as the association has all the power and makes all the rules.

Single family homes can be purchased relatively inexpensively and sold quickly if necessary. You can purchase one house at a time or buy a lot of them if you have the resources. I've found that managing these types of properties produces the best income at the lowest cost.

If, after reviewing this book and other information, you decide to manage your own property, I would recommend that you find an on-site manager, aka a vetted tenant, who will take care of the little things that crop up on a regular basis.

The legalities and liabilities of property management must be completely understood. Always work within the law, as these legal systems were designed to protect the people. The best course of action, if you decide to self-manage, is to do things above board and keeping excellent records. Work within the government guidelines and understand the regulations. Managing your property will be much easier if you are always on the right side of the law.

In order to protect yourself, the best thing you can do is put a barrier between you (the property owner) and the renters. This shields you from liability issues and allows you to sleep better because you don't have to deal with every little grievance such as a plumbing call or tenant noise disturbance.

If you do decide to hire a property management company, don't just hire the first one you find. Investigate several of them. Look at their rate sheets to get an idea of how they charge for their services and learn how they make money before making a decision.

The rate sheet is extremely informative and should be scrutinized and analyzed thoroughly.

- Do they nickel and dime you for every work order?
- Do you get charged for small things like postage stamps and faxes?
- What do they charge for preparing a home to rent?
- Are there fees for advertising for new tenants?
- Are they willing to guarantee the property is rented?

There are many other questions to ask as you look over their rates and services. Get all of your concerns and questions answered to your satisfaction before making any decision. Of course, ensure any agreements are in writing.

In addition to reviewing their rate sheet, examine the systems they use and ensure these do what you need. Look at how many properties they have available to rent at any one time; they should have most units filled most of the time.

The ratio of properties to managers is important. A good manager should be able to handle about a hundred properties as long as good systems are in place. If the management company does not have systems in place, they will struggle, tenants will suffer, errors will occur and profits will be sporadic.

On a final note, one of the very best ways to shield yourself from the liabilities and problems of managing property is to create a master lease agreement. This allows your property management company to lease the property from you, and then rent or lease it out themselves. This effectively isolates you from any liability issues.

Bibliography

Associated Press. (2009, Jul 2). *Child Dies After Being Strangled by Pet Python in Florida.* Retrieved from Fox News: http://www.foxnews.com/story/2009/07/02/child-dies-after-being-strangled-by-pet-python-in-florida/.

Examiner. (2014, Jul 20). *Tampa area child mauled to death by dogs he may have let out of their cages.* Retrieved from Examiner: http://www.examiner.com/article/tampa-area-child-mauled-to-death-by-dogs-he-may-have-let-out-of-their-cages.

Justia U.S. Law. (2012, Jun 21). *Benningfield v. Zinsmeister.* Retrieved from Justia U.S. Law: http://law.justia.com/cases/kentucky/supreme-court/2012/2009-sc-000660-dg.html.

Roger Fisher, W. U. (2011). *Getting to Yes.* Penguin Books.

Thank you to the following who have truly influenced my success

www.DavidTilney.com

www.GaryJohnston.com

www.JohnSchaub.com

www.PeterFortunato.com

Need a Florida Rental Lease, visit:
www.evict.com

For information or for speaking
events with the author, visit:
www.MattFonk.com